# OUT OF THE

How Lotte Reiniger Made

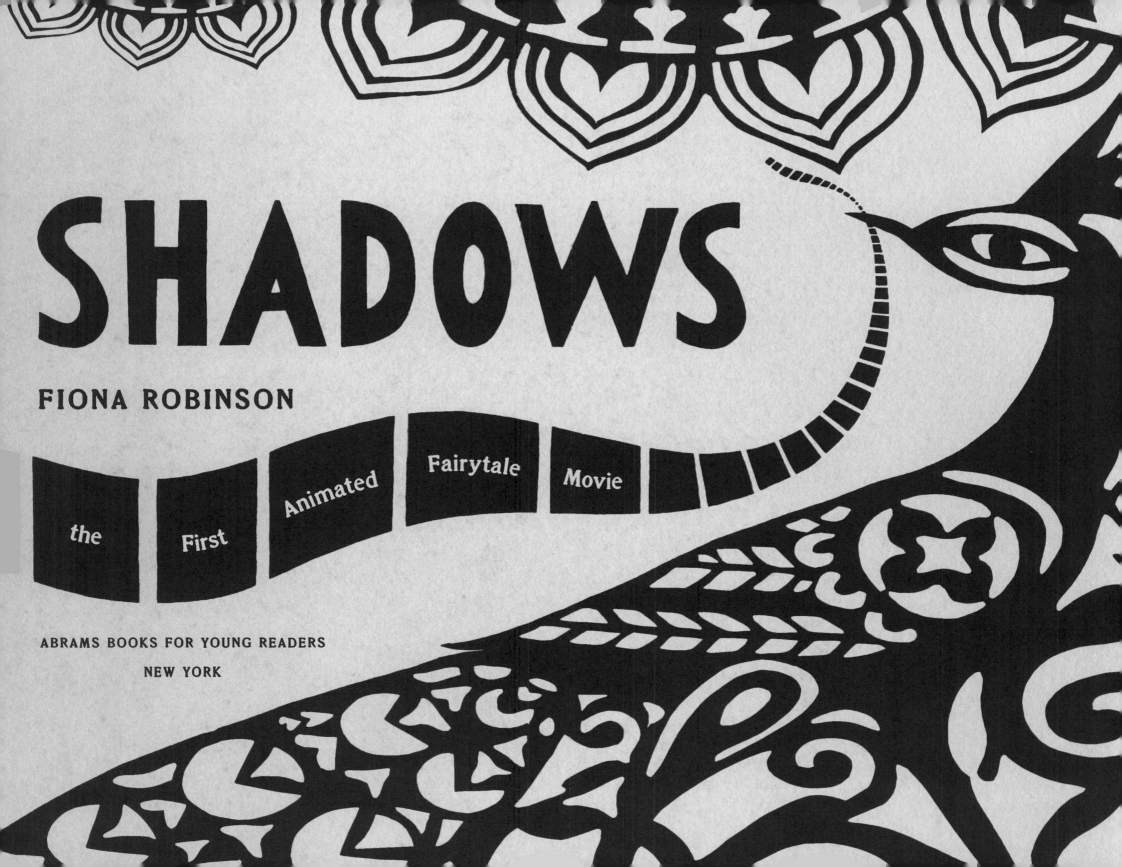

# SHADOWS

FIONA ROBINSON

the First Animated Fairytale Movie

ABRAMS BOOKS FOR YOUNG READERS

NEW YORK

Once upon a time

in Berlin . . . .

. . . there was a little girl who
loved fairytales.

Lotte wandered through deep forests,
spying witches and wolves. She danced
with princesses. She met a frog that was
really a prince, and she spun straw into
gold. There was magic and adventure
everywhere, on every page she turned.

And when she was finally exhausted and
laid down for a nap, *Grimm's Fairy Tales*
slept too, its characters frozen in the precise
moment the book was closed, waiting to
come to life again.

Lotte craved stories like other children craved iced gingerbread. Her parents and grandparents read to her for hours on end. She was their only child and grandchild, and they invested all their hopes in her future happiness. Though Lotte wasn't a fairytale princess, she was *their* princess.

They read and read, until she started to read all by herself.

But Lotte did not live in a fairytale land of long ago. She was born on June 2, 1899, in Germany's largest city, Berlin. And as she grew, so did her country, with life-changing new technologies. If you gazed down to Knesebeck Street below the Reiniger family's small apartment, a prince more likely travelled by car than by storybook steed.

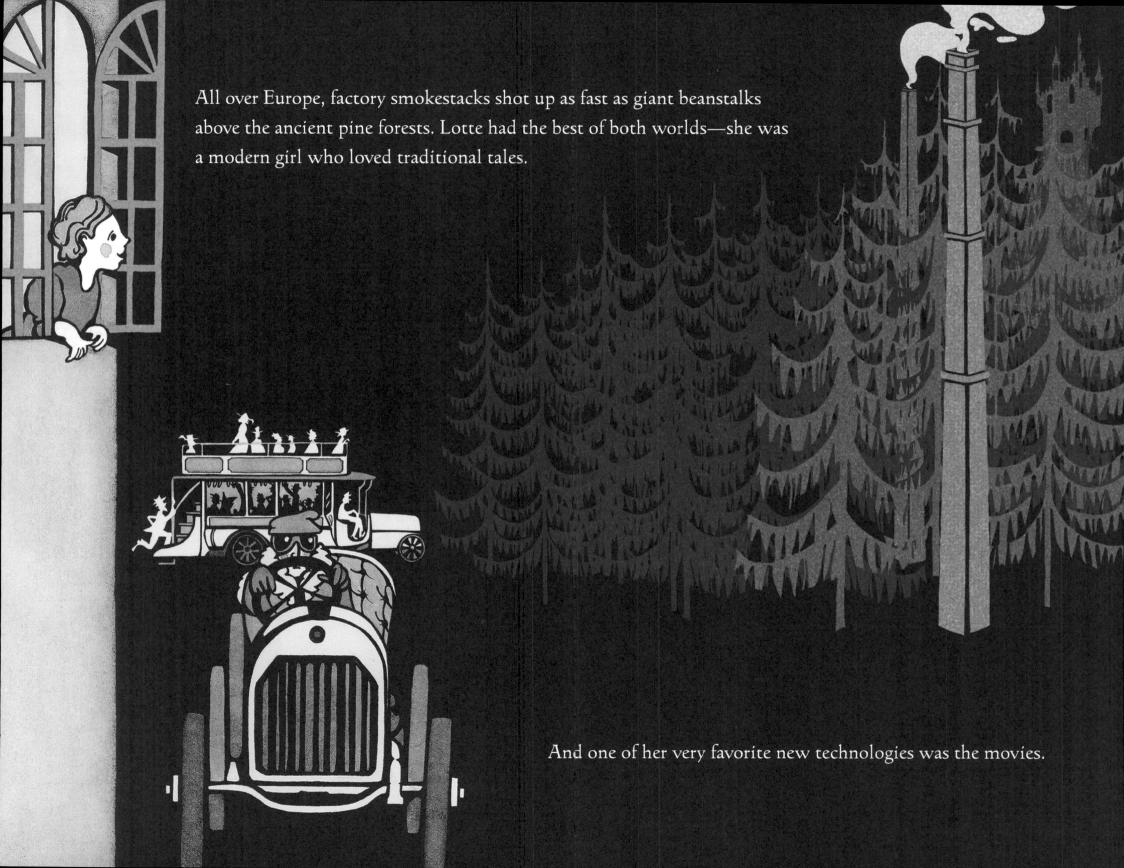

All over Europe, factory smokestacks shot up as fast as giant beanstalks above the ancient pine forests. Lotte had the best of both worlds—she was a modern girl who loved traditional tales.

And one of her very favorite new technologies was the movies.

Her grandmother often took her to the cinema. Lotte especially loved to lose herself in the fantasy films of French director George Méliès. Around 1906, they went to see his *A Trip to the Moon*.

At this time, movies were silent, so a real orchestra would play along with the movie. Just imagine the clash of cymbals as the rocket landed *SPLAT!* in the moon's eye. Méliès made fantasy stories look and sound believable, transporting the audience to a different world!

One day, Lotte was given a gift that would transform her from a *reader* and *viewer* of stories into a *teller* of stories. Chinese puppets allowed Lotte to physically perform her beloved fairytales.

Like a fairy casting a spell with her wand, Lotte flicked her wrist and brought the sleeping puppets to life. Swooping down low, stretching up high, she led them in a dance around the room.

At school, Lotte learned the
traditional craft of Scherenschnitte,
which means "scissor cuts." She
quickly learned that she could create
her own magical papercut characters
from a simple piece of paper!

She snipped away for hours, turning the paper
this way and that, until she was left with
silhouettes and a tiny pile of

paper snow.

But Lotte soon became frustrated with her still papercuts. She wanted them to move and come ALIVE!

Inspired by her Chinese puppets, she turned the papercuts into puppets. Using heavier paper, she connected body parts with wire hinges, mimicking real, fluid movement.

At the age of twelve, she made her own theater from old cardboard boxes. She started to stage plays in her living room, like Shakespeare's *Romeo and Juliet*.

But Lotte wanted a bigger audience: EVERYONE!

As Lotte grew, so did her fascination with cinema. Already bowled over by Méliès' work, she started to enjoy German movies, especially those starring the actor Paul Wegener.

Wegener was very famous, but he wasn't exactly your typical handsome film star.

A giant of a man at six-and-a-half feet tall, he loved to play the roles of monsters and mad scientists. He also directed his own movies and led a troupe of actors. Lotte was his greatest fan.

One day in April 1916, at the age of seventeen, Lotte set off to attend his lecture "New Goals of Cinema."

She entered the theater and sat down.

Wegener started to speak . . .

*We are entering a new pictorial fantasy world as we would enter a magic forest . . .*

Wegener spoke with passion, especially about ANIMATION. He believed that animation could be used to "see before our very eyes a world of pure fantasy come to life."

Lotte was in awe. She didn't want to just *watch* movies, she wanted to *make* them. She raced home and pleaded with her parents to let her study acting at the nearby school where Wegener's troupe was based. She dreamed she might become part of that exciting circle of artists. These were *her people*.

Lotte bloomed at the school. Acting helped build her confidence.

When out of class, she sat and observed Wegener's troupe. Sometimes she was given small roles in his plays and movies. But more often, she would take paper and scissors and create silhouettes of the actors. In return, the troupe would observe her, spellbound by her talent. And they bought the papercuts.

That money helped pay for her tuition and rent. Her tiny, clever snips of paper magically made cash appear! She had the smart idea of creating many, many papercuts of Wegener. She knew this would both flatter him and reveal her talent. And sure enough, Wegener noticed her!

Excited to discover Lotte's remarkable gift, Wegener asked her to join his film crew.
He took Lotte under his mighty wings as her mentor.

One of her first jobs was to make intertitles for his latest movie, *The Mountain Spirit's Wedding*.

**Intertitles**

**were used in the early days of movies . . .**

**because sound in cinema hadn't been invented yet!**

**Intertitles described speech,**

**a change of scene,**

**a loud noise!**

**BOOM!**

**Impressed by her hard work and enthusiasm,**

**Wegener asked Lotte to assist in more films—**

**to design sets,**

# Hark!

# Here comes

# the Pied Piper!

*(But where are the rats? And why are there so
many confused guinea pigs in the street?)*

*The Pied Piper of Hamelin* is the tale of a town plagued by rats. It's a *horrific* fairytale, so *of course* Wegener wanted to make it into a movie! He took the main role as the Piper. In the story, the Piper leads the rats of Hamelin away with his hypnotic flute melody. When the townsfolk refuse to pay the Piper, he lures the town's children away to disappear forever.

Ready to shoot a scene, Lotte hid out of view of the camera with the other crew members. Each crew member had a basket of rats!

At the signal, a gunshot fired,

and the crew released the rats into the street . . .

but the rats ran away.

The rats didn't magically follow Wegener. They disappeared into the town, plaguing the townsfolk.

Next, the crew tried guinea pigs, painted gray with tails attached. A gunshot was fired into the air. The camera whirred. The guinea pigs were released. Wegener turned to see the little creatures in the middle of the street, chewing their fake tails off.

So . . . how to create the magic of hypnotized rats following the Piper?

Wegener asked Lotte to create an animation. Her first! The technique she would use is called STOP MOTION ANIMATION. Using wooden rats, she would convey rats scuttling, scampering, pouring into the streets. A river of rodents drawn to their deaths!

And this is how she did it:

One morning, she and the other crew members hid again along the street, this time each with a basket of wooden rats.

At the signal, they moved the rats onto the street. The movie camera took one shot, called a *frame*, like a single photograph.

Then the rats were moved again, a tiny amount, *incrementally*, and another frame was shot.

With Lotte's direction, this process was repeated many, many thousands of times. It was painstaking work, requiring great patience.

Shooting the frames took all day.

But when the thousands of frames were run together and combined with footage of Wegener prancing along playing the pipe, their hard work was complete.

At the cinemas, audiences LOVED *The Pied Piper of Hamelin*, and *especially* Lotte's rat sequence. By creating this animation, Lotte had become a sorcerer! She had brought the wooden rats to life and enchanted audiences with her animation magic! The movie played for over forty weeks on the German cinema circuit.

Wegener was pleased with Lotte's work. He decided to introduce her to some important people.

Wegener introduced Lotte to Hans Cürliss and Carl Koch, the directors of a new animation studio. Lotte was offered a job, and she eagerly accepted it!

Carl showed Lotte how to use an important piece of animation equipment, the Tricktisch ("trick / animation table"). She began by making several animations with Carl.

Before long, she started to work on her own story using her silhouettes.

She created a plot. She drew a storyboard showing sketches of key moments in her five-minute-long animation. She cut and hinged characters. And she sat at the Tricktisch for hours on end, making incremental movements as Carl shot each frame from above. The film was then dyed with special ink to make the animation colorful.

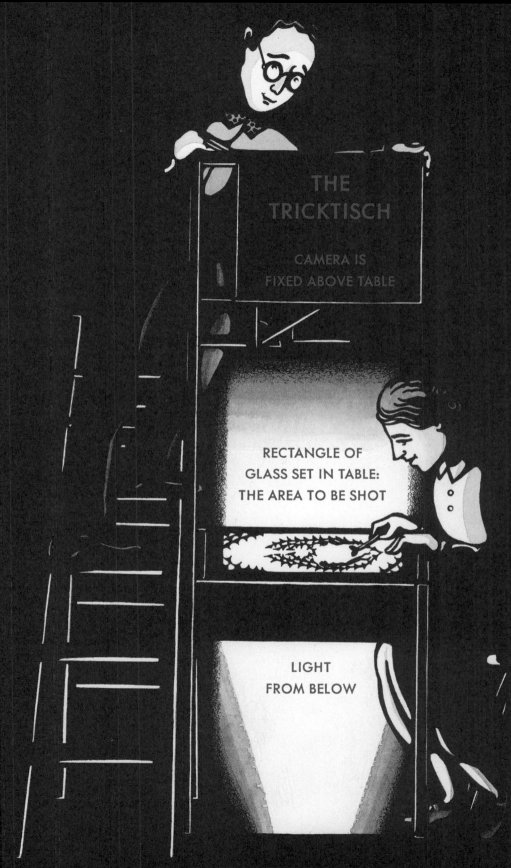

THE TRICKTISCH

CAMERA IS FIXED ABOVE TABLE

RECTANGLE OF GLASS SET IN TABLE: THE AREA TO BE SHOT

LIGHT FROM BELOW

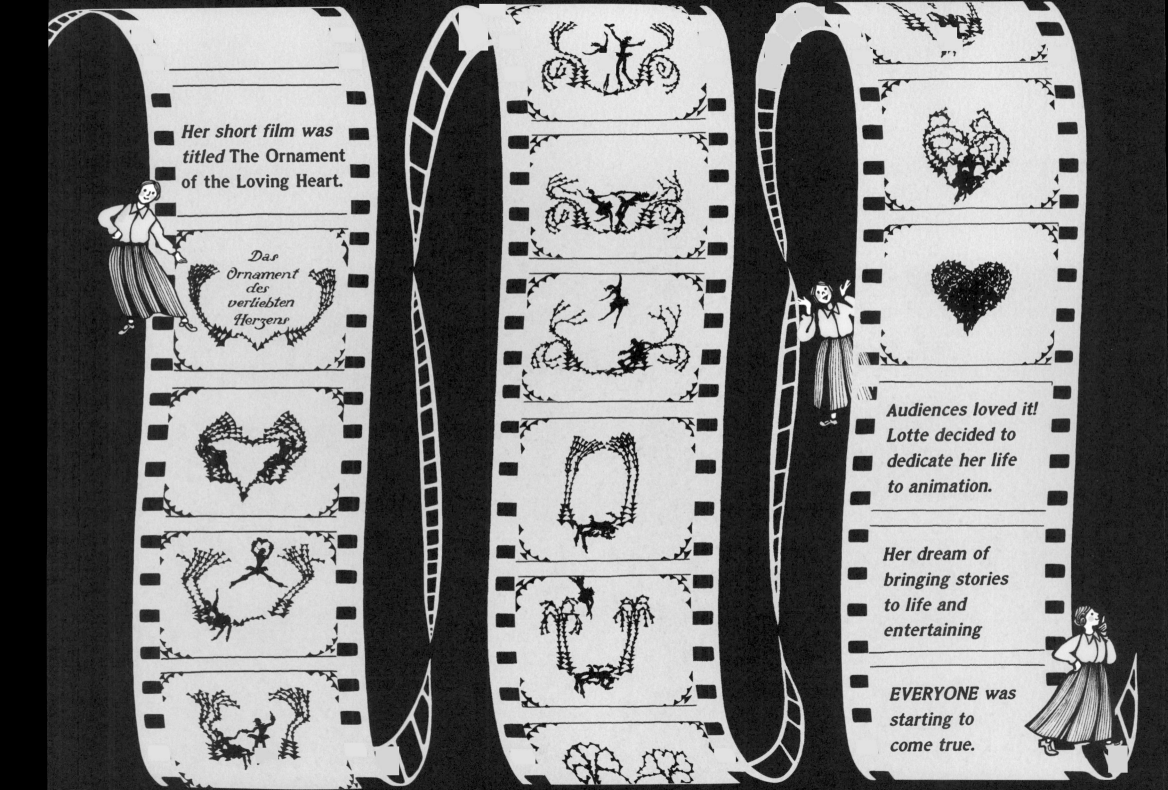

Her short film was *titled* **The Ornament of the Loving Heart.**

*Das Ornament des verliebten Herzens*

**Audiences loved it! Lotte decided to dedicate her life to animation.**

*Her dream of bringing stories to life and entertaining*

**EVERYONE was starting to come true.**

Between 1918 and 1926, after the success of *The Ornament of the Loving Heart*, Lotte's work flowed like a reel of film. She created fairytales such as *Cinderella*, and short cinema advertisements for ink, chocolate, and skin products. All were created with the help of Carl. She was the artist, he the technician. They happily worked together in friendship and with great respect for each other's talents.

And they also fell in love . . .

They were married on December 6, 1921, four years after they first met. And though they would live *happily ever after*, like a fairytale princess and her Prince Charming, they still had work to do and stories to tell!

Lotte wanted to create more convincing animations by getting a feel for a creature's movement "in her bones." When not at the studio working with Carl, she attended the ballet and visited the Berlin Zoo. Observing the animals and copying them, Lotte would attract an audience of giggling children. She didn't mind one bit!

Then one day in 1923, a handsome stranger arrived at the institute. He approached Lotte and Carl. His name was Louis Hagen, a wealthy banker and arts patron.

*He had an idea.*

*He wanted to know if Lotte would make a full-length silhouette animation film!*

*This had never been done before!*

*Lotte later said, "Animated films were supposed to make people roar with laughter, and nobody had dared entertain an audience with them for more than ten minutes."*

She felt unsettled, muddled by both excitement and worry. Lotte had always dreamed of making a longer movie, but it simply cost too much. At the time, there was widespread poverty in Germany. But Hagen had invested in a huge amount of unused film. And, because this was a most depressing era for most Germans, Hagen thought that they would want to escape real life at the movies.

It was an offer she could not refuse!

# Part Three
## 1923–1926

# The sorcerer
# casts her spell!

*(in a tiny attic, above a garage in Potsdam)*

Lotte chose to take her viewers on a journey away from Germany, inspired by *1,001 Arabian Nights*. The tales collected in this volume drew from many different storytelling traditions, including Arabic, Turkish, Greek, Jewish, Indian, and Persian.

Lotte decided to weave together several stories for maximum fantasy. There would be flying horses, evil sorcerers, witches and demons, explosions and storms—all great subjects for experimenting with special effects. The title would be *The Adventures of Prince Achmed.*

Louis Hagen offered her a studio: an attic above a garage at his country home. Lotte hired four animators to help with her massive endeavor. Lotte, Carl, and their team moved to Potsdam to work on the film.

There was so much for Lotte to do! She created a story outline and character sketches. Then she made storyboards. Each animator was given specific tasks and encouraged to experiment with anything the team could afford! The cheapest of household materials—soap, paint, sand, and wax—would be used to create the most magical special effects. She also hired a composer named Wolfgang Zeller to create a musical score to play along with the movie.

She created her characters and background landscapes using thin lead and, often, old diaper boxes! Most of the time, she knelt on an old car seat, which she found most comfortable. And, of course, she had to spend many long hours making tiny incremental movements of her characters as Carl shot each frame.

Lotte had to juggle many different things!

Lotte's previous animations were beautiful, but quite flat in appearance. To make the backgrounds appear more distant, Lotte figured she could use a Tricktisch with many glass plates, not just one, stacked below the camera. Such a camera would add a greater sense of depth to her fantasies, and with this many-layered, super-tall Tricktisch, multiple animators could work at the same time. As such a thing did not exist, Lotte had to invent it!

Her invention became known as the world's first MULTIPLANE CAMERA.

The team worked hard, putting in long days in their tiny workspace.

Sometimes, Lotte was weighed down by doubts. She worried that an audience wouldn't sit through an hour-long animated movie, that she'd taken on too much, that she'd fail.

But with Carl's support and her hard determination, she carried on.

Finally, after three years of living and breathing *The Adventures of Prince Achmed*, the movie was finished! The movie was 65 minutes long. They had shot 250,000 frames, of which 96,000 were used!

Like many artists who commit to a lengthy process, they feared no one would show up to the premiere. They handwrote over 8,000 invitations to get the word out. And they prepared themselves for disappointment.

Premiere of
THE ADVENTURES OF
PRINCE ACHMED
Sunday, May 2, 1926
Volksbühne Theater, Berlin

The big day arrived.

Lotte awoke, disappointed to see the sun shining.
Surely after a hard winter, folks would want to
be outside, not in a dark cinema.

As she and Carl approached the theater,
they were shocked to see a long line of people.
Pushing through the crowds inside, Lotte saw
Zeller warming up his orchestra.

She watched as arguments broke out over seats.
People filled the aisles and grew restless waiting.

At last, *The Adventures of Prince Achmed*

lit the screen . . .

The audience was hooked.

The theater was so packed that the police arrived, worried about the crowd's safety. But Lotte persuaded them to let the show go on!

Lotte raced around looking for the fire and discovered sacks that had been left to dry on heaters were smoldering. The cinema crew hadn't noticed—they were too absorbed in the movie.

As the movie reached its grand finale, Lotte noticed smoke billowing up the screen! The audience thought it was a special effect and was not frightened.

When the film ended, the crowd went wild with appreciation!

With her dream come to life, Lotte stepped out of the shadows, and took a bow.

*The Adventures of Prince Achmed* took its place in film history as the first full-length fairytale movie. It is also considered the oldest surviving full-length animation. For a young woman in 1926, this is a remarkable, almost unbelievable achievement. But all of this is true, and absolutely not a fairy story!

Lotte would go on to make many, many more movies—and to have many more adventures with Carl. Future animators would be greatly inspired by her pioneering work, her unique silhouette style, and her mesmerizing, magical movies.

So, let us now end her story so she can enjoy a nap in her palace of imagination. Lotte Reiniger, the Queen of Animation, is always waiting for you to revisit.

# AUTHOR'S NOTE

Lotte led a full, fascinating life. It was difficult to contain all her adventures in these forty-eight pages, so I focused on her experiences, art, and innovations that lead up to *The Adventures of Prince Achmed*. Here's a little of what happened to Lotte subsequently.

After the premiere in Berlin, *The Adventures of Prince Achmed* had its French premiere in Paris in 1926, where she met the famous French director Jean Renoir. Lotte, Carl, and Renoir became great friends, and Carl frequently worked on technical aspects of Renoir's movies. The iconic German director Fritz Lang, who had attended the Berlin premiere, was also impressed by Lotte's talent and asked her to create an animation for his pioneering science fiction movie *Metropolis* (1927).

Throughout Germany in the 1920s and '30s, a political storm was brewing. The Nazi Party rose to power, whose doctrines both Lotte and Carl opposed. They decided to leave their country in 1935. Many of their Jewish friends and colleagues, including composer Wolfgang Zeller, had already fled to avoid persecution and imprisonment. Lotte and Carl went to England, France, and Italy, working in each country until their visas ran out, then moving onto the next. In September 1939, Great Britain, France, and Poland declared war on Germany after the Germans invaded Poland. World War II had begun.

In December 1943, Lotte received the news that her mother, still living in Berlin, was seriously ill, partly due to a food shortage. So Lotte and Carl returned to look after her, although they were afraid for their lives.

Lotte was forced to start work on an animation for the regime, which she did reluctantly and as slowly as possible so it couldn't be completed. She was paid with a meager amount of food vouchers to survive on. During the Battle of Berlin, she hid in a basement and an underground shaft as the city crumbled. She hung papercuts in local bookshops for friends to see, to show that she was still alive.

World War II ended in 1945. In 1949, Lotte and Carl moved to the United Kingdom. Both of them suffered from exhaustion and illness due to malnutrition from the war, Carl especially. They began their new lives making animations for the General Post Office and the BBC. Lotte's stop frame animations greatly inspired the work of the BBC's remarkable, much-loved early childhood animations of the 1950s and '60s.

After a few years, Lotte and Carl came across an old friend—Louis Hagen's son (also named Louis Hagen), who was a refugee in London. Louis decided to set up an animation production company for them in 1952. It was named Primrose Productions. Louis Hagen Jr. gave Lotte a new Tricktisch and set up a studio in London. She created thirteen animations for American television by 1954, and this became the most productive period of her life.

In 1962, Lotte and Carl became British citizens. But Carl never recovered from the malnutrition he had suffered in the 1940s, and in 1963, he died. Lotte said, "It is terrible my husband is gone, because you cannot imagine a better partner in the world." Lotte withdrew from the world and stopped animating, only occasionally advising on her old love—puppetry.

Lotte stepped out of the shadows of grief slowly. By the 1970s, her animations were being revived, and people took great interest in her technique and achievements. She began touring the world, giving talks on her career. She wrote an excellent book, *Shadow Puppets, Shadow Theatres, and Shadow Films* (1970), which included instructions on making many useful things, including a Tricktisch! And she continued her animations, the last being *The Four Seasons* in 1980.

On June 19, 1981, while staying with friends in Tübingen, Germany, Lotte died in her sleep. She is buried in Dettenhausen, Germany, next to her beloved Carl.

But Lotte's legacy lives on in the many homages that grateful animators have made to her and her work. In *Fantasia* (1940), a silhouetted Mickey Mouse is interspliced with live-action musicians, a reference to Lotte's technique. The 2004 movie *Lemony Snicket's A Series of Unfortunate Events* mimics Lotte's style in its credits. In the "Tale of the Three Brothers" sequence in *Harry Potter and the Deathly Hallows—Part 1* (2010), her influence can clearly be seen.

The director and creator of the animated television series *Steven Universe*, Rebecca Sugar, made an homage to Lotte in the episode *The Answer* (2016). Sugar said, "A lot of *Steven Universe* crew members were hugely inspired by Lotte Reiniger's work."

## A NOTE ABOUT *THE ADVENTURES OF PRINCE ACHMED*

Please be aware that *The Adventures of Prince Achmed* was intended for adult viewing. At this time in history, animated movies were not specifically created for children. Lotte's movie contains some frightening, violent, and sexual scenes, and her heroes and heroines comply to the gender stereotypes of the time and to the stories on which they were based.

Her movie can also be viewed as an example of orientalism: This is the exaggerated, imagined Western depiction of Middle Eastern, South Asian, and East Asian cultures, resulting in stereotyping and exoticism. Later in the 1950s, recognizing the harmfulness of stereotypes, Lotte changed the way she interpreted different ethnicities.

## LOTTE REINIGER MOVIES SUITABLE FOR CHILDREN

*The Ornament of the Loving Heart* (1919)
*Cinderella* (1922)
*Puss in Boots* (1934)
*Thumbelina* (1955)

## BIBLIOGRAPHY


Blattner, Evamarie, Bernd Desinger, Matthias Knop, Wiebke Ratzeburg, eds. *Lotte Reiniger: Filmstills*. Tübingen: Wasmuth, 2015.

Blattner, Evamarie, and Karlheinz Wiegmann. *Lotte Reiniger: Born with Enchanting Hands: Three Silhouette Sequels*. Tübingen: Wasmuth, 2010.

Dulcken, Henry William. *Dalziel's Illustrated Arabian Nights Entertainments*. London: Ward, Lock & Tyler, 1865.

Grace, Whitney. *Lotte Reiniger: Pioneer of Film Animation*. Jefferson, NC: McFarland & Company, 2017.

Pilling, Jayne. *Women & Animation: A Compendium*. London: British Film Institute, 1992.

Reiniger, Lotte. *Shadow Puppets, Shadow Theatres, and Shadow Films*. Boston, MA: Plays, Inc., 1970.


## FILM

There is a short documentary film by Primrose Productions called *The Art of Lotte Reiniger* (1970) that I thoroughly recommend, especially for young animators. In it, Lotte shows her sketches, storyboards, characters, and her masterful, super-speedy scissor technique. It is also wonderful to hear her jolly, down-to-earth voice. At one point she advises animators to cut a hole in their dining room table to make their own Tricktisch!

## INSTITUTIONS

Institutions holding examples of Lotte's art, artifacts, and archives:

- British Film Institute, London, UK
- Filmmuseum Düsseldorf, Düsseldorf, Germany
- Max Reinhardt Archives and Library, Binghamton University, New York, USA
- Stadtmuseum Tübingen, Tübingen, Germany

Please check that Lotte's work is on display before planning your trip!

## ILLUSTRATION CREDITS

All images are created by the illustrator with the following based on original art as indicated below: **Cover:** Flying horse based on Lotte's from *The Adventures of Prince Achmed* (1926). **Back cover:** Lotte's hand and scissors are based on a still from *Cinderella* (1922). Her signature is based on the intertitle that introduced many of her animations. **Title page:** Peacock design based on Lotte's title design for *The Adventures of Prince Achmed.* **Page 10:** Screen image based on *A Trip to the Moon* directed by Georges Méliès (1902). **Page 16:** Papercuts (actors only) based on Lotte's originals (1917–1919). The original papercuts are held in the Max Reinhardt Archives and Library. **Pages 26, 38, 39, 40, 41:** Film stills are based on *The Ornament of the Loving Heart* (1919) and *The Adventures of Prince Achmed*, both directed by Lotte. **Page 31:** Arabian Nights characters based on those from *Dalziel's Illustrated Arabian Nights' Entertainments* (1865). **Pages 32, 33:** Characters, willow leaves, and gazebo based on Lotte's originals from *The Adventures of Prince Achmed.* **Pages 42, 43:** Characters in trees and sky are based on Lotte's animated characters (1919–1980).

## ACKNOWLEDGMENTS


Huge thanks to Jay Zukerkorn, Paul Rodeen, Erica Finkel, Amy Vreeland, Heather Kelly, and Alison Gervais. Also, I am very grateful to the British Film Institute for helping with my research.


***For Jay***


The illustrations were created using scissor-cut silhouette, watercolors, and felt pen.

Cataloging-in-Publication Data has been applied for and may be obtained from the Library of Congress.

ISBN 978-1-4197-4085-5





Book design by Heather Kelly





Printed and bound in China

10 9 8 7 6 5 4 3 2 1

**ABRAMS** The Art of Books
195 Broadway, New York, NY 10007
abramsbooks.com

THE